Space Between the Crescent Shadows

One lover's account...

ANDREY PSYCHE

ISBN-13: 978-1-79-262723-1

DEDICATION

To all of my loved ones, whether friends or family, thank you for your daily support, encouragement and acceptance of everything that I am and everything that I am becoming. You mean everything to me!

And to my love, whom I can feel behind the scenes, thank you for inspiring me to become the person that I am today. Each day I find myself reaching and striving for more, so that I could be the man I know you deserve to have in your life.

This world knows no measure of the love I have for you.

CONTENTS

SPACE

The gust that butterfly's wings must create to thrust itself an inch or two can send a particle of dew to tumble downwards to the ground and get absorbed by your favorite flower

The sound an ant makes when he screams can tremble a vibrant beetles wings enough so that when it takes off, it veers off to one side so much that when it lands, your shoulder is the only place that it can reach, sharing its colors

A simple greeting down the road that took a second, not much more, would leave a string of pleasure, sing a song of leisure to a being that would walk by cheerfully right next to you and smile and gleam so that a little bit of love would shine your way in case today would be the day you're feeling down

An ocean might be separating us but don't you worry oh my love, I have all that I need to be right next to you

Whether the weather or a bug that hears my prayers from up above or down below would break the mold just by an inch and shift the universe just so

So by the time it got to you my presence irrefutable, immutably bring just a bit of comfort in ungodly hours that carries hope and starry eyes, look at the moon oh just one more time before the sandman hand arrives and you can rest your head on mine inside our dreams in which you're mine and I

am yours, combined unknowingly before the day that I can set
The world back down from off my chest
To breath you in and drift away
To see you in another day
Forever yours
My name

So many things that I could do to chase you down and be with you
to crawl, control the threads that bind us
Pull on the matrix lies behind us
I've learned the ways of snake before me and used them freely, end of story
I used them times I saw you last
For my desires to have passed
I used them or perhaps they me
To taint a perfect little seed
But I ran scared for rightful reasons
I did not want to hurt you more
Just like I did with them before
Intentions paved the road to hell
And I've been working day and night
Been wearing colors on the side
Bright neon orange reflects the sky
No more
No more
Don't want to stoop down to the floor
Might not be manly to allow the world to bring you to my door but I have
made my wanting you right next to me quite clear I hope 'cus I don't want
to
Manipulate you in any way shape or form to get you
No flattery, no urging, no nagging, no demands
Just my heart waiting for the taking
Laying open in my hands
Pulsating, beating, longing, yearning
If you should take it, please be warned
The love burns hot, it might just scold you
But you must choose it on your own
I cannot play a part in your decision
I cannot force your hand one bit
It must be your exercise of freedom
To dive in flames of scorching heat
I really hope to see you wander around my corner of the woods
Because this waiting would feel like torture, yet, it is a sweet nectar on my
lips
It cries and cries just for a glance
I know the universe got plans but if for once you crave a chance
I'll show you worlds you can attain by grabbing embers
From
My
Tongue

3

Up through the chest
Where it originally sparked
To weld a fissure in my heart
A fissure bleeding on and on and on
I feel it now, it makes me moan
The pain won't stop
Nor do I want it
Just want it to kick up a notch
Tear me apart
Just need your help
I'll wait
and wait
and wait
and wait
'Til you give in to ring that bell

Heart longs for love
The touch of your skin
Caress of your gaze
Up and down my essence
The heart throbs needle pain
Penetrating through the skin
Out the rib cage dwells again
Open for the world to see
Doesn't bother me a bit
Air it out
And get it out
And tear it out
'Cus it wants to be within
Your insides
Inside YOUR skin
Alongside its equal mass
Cuddled up as close as atoms
Separation inconceivable
Pain and pleasure felt in unison
Beating rhythmically
Beating still

Sitting on a rock, listening to the water rush beside me, couldn't help but see an image in my mind, an image of you, in all the shapes and all the forms and all the faces that you've inhabited. All the pain you've put me through and all the glory in the end. I couldn't help but sing a song to capture all of the events in mind and hope you heard just but a word so I can sleep tonight in knowing that my voice is heard a thousand miles or round the bend wherever you chose to hide out.

Internal struggles flow throughout
No wonder you denied the drought
I saw the river flowing strong
Jumped in
Got wet
And stayed abroad
No wonder you found freedom in
The loss of contact
The loss of steam
It's simple
Short
And to the point
No need for make up to destroy
The beauty of how nature works
The beauty of perfections faults
To choose our roles
To truly be
Whatever we desire
Whatever we believe
And know that when the tine grows near
You'd see the truth
We shed the fear
And with it reinvent the thought
Of how two souls begin to bond

The symbols all around my eyes
Combine together to form a prize
A time, a place, a vibrant scene
Of you and I, a winning team
Success, in body, mind and heart
Tall fortunes, blessed us from the start
Ahead we stare, with gazes fierce
Progression forward, in mind new wins
Through marriage of the psyche
The right and left combine
Abundance in our heart and soul
The only factor, time
Plant seeds of love and happiness
In fertile grounds within
My mind is full of wonder
My thoughts are simply, WIN
Entranced in silence, Victoria and I
Eyes locked together, our hearts undoubtedly combine
The magic of true love is blinding
It stops the public, froze in time
With possibilities galore
You take my hand, and I take yours
A million choices, a billion doors
Each one a promise, a life of more
The sharpest weapon ever forged
Trajectory of you and I defined
With pin point focus, strength and will
A richer feast doth not been dined
With juices flowing and stars aligned
Our day approaches, Victory in mind

Can't make you happy
Can't give you love
'Cus you must have it in YOUR heart
Have zero power over you
Only myself and all I do
I'll chose to make myself complete
You do the same and then we'll meet
You will not find your missing piece
You have to mold it, through blazing heat

Take my hand and we'll get lost
Whirlwind of colors all around us
The sun will wink each coming day
We'll shine together, absorb each ray
Reanimate our frozen hearts
Reacclimate to loves warm touch
Retaliate to lonesome nights
Respond, Remember and Reignite
To finally feel a breath of ease
To know you're hers and she is his
And worry not of future days
Because for you, there's only faith

In love that led you to this spot
In the emotion of your heart
In the desire of you two
To be the ones, to be them true
She never makes you change a thing
You're who she loves and strives to win
He wouldn't dare to love her less
For anytime, her heart undress
Reanimate the true loves flames
Reacclimate to worlds unchained
Retaliate to time and space
Return, Recharge and Reembrace

No other girl could take your place
Perhaps your daughter but let's not haste
Our souls to grow and intertwine
Our hearts to merge and love turn blind
For all our planets to align
Live in our dream, get lost in time
To finally feel a breath of ease
To know you're hers and she is his
And worry not of future days
Because for you, there's only faith

I'll promise you the world
And bring it to your knees
I'll promise you a love
That makes your body weak
I'll promise you a fire
That burns you from within
I'll promise you reality
Surpass your wildest dreams
One thing I could not promise
No matter how I try
No matter my desire
Or willingness or might
This thing I cannot promise
You probably won't like
As much as I would love to
I'm never one To lie
Can't promise you tomorrow
Regardless how you want it
Can't guarantee you futures
Cus all we've got is this moment
I'll promise you my heart
Do with it as you may
I'll promise you my strength
Protect you and be brave
I'll promise you the nurture
You've craved for all your life
I'll promise you all this and more
Without demands or fights
One thing I could not promise
No matter how I try
No matter my desire
Or willingness or might
This thing I cannot promise
You probably won't like
As much as I would love to
I'm never one To lie
Can't promise you tomorrow
I'm sorry but it's true
Can't guarantee you futures
But now, it's all for you
Right now, it's all for you
Right here and now it's all for you

Two hearts mirroring each other
Every want and every need
Doesn't matter if they gather water or dis-ease
Longing for it brings the former
Latter pleases boisterous feet
When you run you never gather
Pictures on the wall to keep

Well at last the ends upon us
Watch the final star take shape
Dressed up to the nines while inside the chamber closes
Chapters open
Clears his throat
The sentence starts
Sit beside me
Look inside me
Let the movie play along
We'll get lost within the hours that would otherwise be gone
Yea I've said a million times
That tonight will be the night
To be frank it is and isn't
Every moment lives and dies
But if I extend this second
Stretch it thin from tail to end
Just perhaps I can imagine
Nor a place, neither a time
That could never really see
And perhaps, that's what I want
Hide inside the fifth dimension
This is where I know you'll be
But for now I'll save a seat
For the infinite and me

Then I start to see
A kind of nudity that's censored from the eyes of man
Internal confidence that doesn't wither or depend on anything or anyone
that looks its way
We are the same but you're not me
You're somebody new
In this world or mockery and mimicry
You stand tall above the sea of faces that once tried to drown me
But no more
Now I'm walking out the door
Leaving you
A snuggly warm burrito in our bed
I promise that
I won't be long
I'll bring you flowers
The ones I grew myself on the driveway just so I could pick the prettiest
one and send it your way
I'll smell them each and every day and on that day that fragrance reaches
sure its perfection
A smell that hints at what you do to me when I can close my eye and dive
inside the rolling waves of ecstasy 'cus all I am is just a fool addicted to your
sweet forbidden fruit
You sprout desires in my soul and buried roots inside my bones so even
when we are apart I feel a part of home, belonging, distant moans that
crawl upon my skin resembling fires that we burn when there's no distances
between
Our fingertips
Ride to the sunset
Wake up at dawn
Stumble on treasures in the dark
And sing a gentle harmony with you and I and my guitar
Share with the world
Our love
Engrave the waves with both our names
Let fickle time stare in this way with awe and taste how immortality slide
past the day to day and finds it buried in the hands of two mortal bodies
That's why we dance
We twirl and chant
And stare so deep into our eyes
And recognize a part of self that sprung to life inside the body of another
Entangled souls finally find each other
To lead a lifestyle bound by growth

To try their best at every turn
To share their journey with the world
To leave the past and build to last millennia to come
Together seeds begin to rise up out of buried darkness and flourish back
into a flower
The nectar that would feed the world
This rose that only grew because you watered it

Smiles and butterflies arise
Within that sparkle in your eyes
As you sat and joyfully declared
How photography is dead
Captured all between the lines
Underneath each color droplet
Painted over by our mind
Yet
It remains so clear and stagnant
Time might win the war at last
But each memory will last
Every heart beat was recorded
Every moment, felt so raw
Every brush stroke brought to life
Things we wanted from afar
It was you who captured people
In the essence on your page
Won their hearts with but a sketchbook
"Please return another day"
They say,
Will you?
Who's to say
But your thoughts will travel daily
There and back 5 times a day
Digging up the feelings buried
By the artist on the page
Life would seem to go forever
Limitations out of sight
Sitting down and paint the picture
Of the light
Bouncing off the things we like
And perhaps one day you'll find me
Dancing up among the stars
Nestled gently with Orion,
Jupiter won't seem so far
Twirling round the Northern Star
and by then all of my songs have faded and my paintings turned to dust
You'll still hear the echoes ringing
Echoes
of the future's past

Along that which is too mundane
I try to change the space and save
The very best of me, for you
It took me time, and yes
It's true that I have faulted many
And yes, I've fallen on my face
I'm beaten, tired, yet I'm standing
Waiting to see you, face to face
I've thrown my heart into the aether
I've sang my songs in the abyss
I've channeled grace and in good spirits
I've sent you kisses and embraced
Each every portion of your being
Each flaw that you may or may not have
I care too much to leave you hanging
I can't coagulate this bleeding heart
Each night the moon is my own postman
He sends you messages at night
It's but one way that I can reach you
For now, I'll miss you in the daylight

Spent a year inside detention,
Carving brick walls in my mind
But today a window opened
Felt the breeze, and smelled the pines
Frolicked in the vibrant meadows
Got distracted purple hues
Kneeled on one knee and proposed
Shall we eat a plum or two?
Yes I feel it
The abundance
Fifty more each time I reach
For a small part of mortality
Slightly staring at deaths feet
Russian jargon keeps me focused as the scarlet letter passed
Four bananas and one orange
That's the price of a tank of gas

The trees will keep us warm at night
The canopy will steel our sight
The moment plight escapes your lips will be the greatest of our lives
This sadness entering our skin
The purge will happen from within
These fingers scout the land ahead
This breath will fly,
Never to return again.
Inside eternity, inside your light
A rescue mission undermined my one ability to thrive within the confines
of my one track mind
Yet I will find
A timeline that has crossed both space and time
One parallel to you and I
And I
Did pluck it from above, I tugged and pulled and yanked and shoved
And down she came, down came my love
She merged our worlds
We joined at last
Now I can look outside once more
And see a string that once was gold
Turn red
And lead without a doubt
I'll follow blindly
All my life

The night could not be colder
Didn't stop be nonetheless
Sat beneath the moon for hours
Just to hear your soul undress
As though the freckles on the surface
Spoke of mysteries within
And the depths of darkest waters
Would bring love to me again
Nothing on this earth could stop me
Golden giant, high on you
You are glistening in the moonlight
Gaia's heart reborn in you
Pulling on these strings so gentle
Lay me down and let me go
Losing you was almost fatal
Falling from that waterfall
Younger still emerge upon us
Be the light you're meant to be
bless us with your hues of darkness
Don't you worry about me
Only after Evie's laughter
May we melt the ice caps free
Will our friendship reignite us
Running to my destiny

A day to remember
No I didn't forget
Every gift that you've sent me
Has been placed on the shelf
Every trophy and ribbon
Each expression alike
Sits atop of the mantle
Radiating your heart
I remember the reasons
I still feel what I feel
That ain't goin' to wither
Distance keeps me estranged
'Cus the shackles I wear now
Are of my own free will
They're the trophies I cherish
It's what taught me these skills
And believe me, I promise
To deliver it, honest
But first I needed healing
To my shock got bombarded
What I tell you this evening
I can surely stand firm
I have seen your reflection
I have felt ghastly colds
Yet, I weathered it graceful
So did you, I could tell
Now there's one thing remaining
I must see you again

You look as fly
As the mountain sky
On a summers eve
When the nightly breeze
Whistling by
Making you slow down, inhale
Exclaim, "Man it's good to be alive"

Have you seen this one before?
The one that keeps on waiting?
Isn't rushed by fools behind her?
Just sits back to watch the sun
Set her standards way too high
You would snicker, call her crazy
Walks alone both too and fro
Stops to smell the growing flowers
Isn't tangled inside time
Just allows the beat to linger
Isn't fazed by public eye
All she wants is to remember
Just a girl and her guitar in between a world of silence
Making music with her heart
It's her tribute to the goddess

Train tracks rattle back and forth
Hear her heart beat past your eardrums

Flowers falling from the sky
Every petal symbolized
Moments that would bring us high
Up the mountains high above
Gently set it at your feet
Love this true knows no defeat
Heart so pure, blind men could see
Feeling of your tender love
Know that I could spend a lifetime
Soaking in your warm embrace
Waking up inside our silence
Always craving one more taste
Thank the heavens that you came
New moons captured our intent
Blessed was the lion when
Taurus started his ascent
And I will lean in one more time
Whispering these words divine
You allowed my heart to shine
Realized the face of beauty
Please remember love of mine
I will always be inside
In your breath and in your eyes
Nights may pass but my love,
My love is forever

Entering my scene
Like a silent movie film
The wind, she made you fly
Through my heart and through my mind
It's as if it all made sense
Every puzzle and every scent
Why my feet were grounded still
After years of restlessness
Swaying back and forth
Running in and out
A flower spun between my fingers
I withstood the drought
You sat in front of me that night
I let it bleed, my heart, she howled
You gazed upon, your eyes, they shined
For but one moment
Stretched oh so thin
Embraced me
Forget again
That after this we'll go our ways
But rest assured
This day, today
Will be engraved, and will be saved
Until the final breath I take

I reach out for a hand
To fill the space between my fingers
You're always there
A smile to share
A cross to bare
Anywhere
I'm always here
After a day of chasing dreams you've always wanted someone in between
your sheets,
Laying, sleeping, keeping space but never weeping
For you
I've always wanted someone to wake up to
To kiss goodbye as your eyes shy away from lights too bright for young
ungodly hours
Leave a note of love behind
While you chased butterflies inside your head
On a pillow that we shared
Just like those nightmares that would eat us up when life would keep us
separate
No longer so
A cat would scurry on the floor
Black fur and whiskers to her toes
Would wake you after I had gone to spread the joy among the young, the
reckless, the confused, the dumb but willing to transform
How much I've grown
The songs I wrote for you still linger in our home
You keep them floating through the air in hums and moans
The air conditioned to the melodies reverberate the walls to sooth the
sleeping toddler woken by imaginary fears
Don't worry
I'll be here
We'll sing you harmonies and whisper in your ear that mom and dad won't
let a single tear fall short
That every miracle brought forth a time and place
Where little feet would grow to big ones
Without the bitter taste that we our self had to embrace until the day that
came to wake us from a slumber and shake us 'til we almost gave up but
never did
Because we saw each other in the mirror
We read the other in our books
And on the radio, TV
And in the clouds

And license plates
And on the billboards that would scream of other nonsense but within each
sentence sparks gave us more than they could see
It was destined, you and me
Music shaped the waves that crunched the universe in ways that shortened
every road and valley
That looped each corner on itself
So that no matter where we traveled
The other one would be in reach
It was that day
That day that smelled like country rain
That day that I forgot my mind and turned around to meet my fate
Eyes locked
Hearts beat in rhythmic pace
Jaws drop and tears begin to race
It came
The day the prophecy left out
Was never written down in stone
But there it was
As real as daylight
The moment ceased to flee , finding its rest
It landed softly in these tired, withered hands
And found a home, nurtured and all
Never to fall short again

I look upon you
The same face
The same expression
The same glow inside your eyes
The same freckles
Same selection of foundation on your cheeks
But for reasons I don't know
The excitement has grown to slow
I'm not flying past my limits
Happy hovering above
Bushes, tree stumps, kissing lovers
But for me, my love, it's enough
Used to send you long emotions
Carving them on every tree
Proving you my deep devotions
Now I see you, and just breathe
I don't hide
I cannot linger
I'm not howling at the moon
I'll just walk and know inside me
That I'll see you back at home
Snuggle closer
All alone
Words can rest inside our silence
Let our hearts embrace the moment
Peace is worth its weight in gold

There is happiness in your eyes that escape the grasp of many
A glimmer of innocence hangs off the tips of your eyelashes
Behind the cornea lies a soul too delicate for this world
It is the pain endured that gave birth to a straight posture and an aromatic
heart
The scars that once bled gave a blades edge to your beauty that intoxicates
with each glance
That is why a glimmer of innocence is so rare to see
A glimmer of hope that screams out for more of the impossible
But
Time has proven to be on our side
And lady luck favors the hopeless romantic

I'll continue in a moment
Recollect my thoughts and start
Reasoning with salty water
To the facts on which I float
Found my hope behind some alley
Took her hand and brought her home
Shook her dry and fed her belly
Now she never feels alone
No one wants to feel alone
There's a coin that rolled between the floorboards in the distance
Listened as the sound so gently stopped in mid chorale
No one would surmise the absent presence of my laughter
The laughter ended when I came back to life
Man it's good to be alive
Question everything that happened
There's a story underneath
All they want is your compliance *Unzips pants* "Get on your knees!"
Toxic people want your essence
They're too weak to make their own
Cut them off and watch them shrivel
Build your energy alone
Build momentum on your own
Once you walk through open portals
You may want to turn on back
Once your eyes are fully open
You can't possibly go blind
Either fight for righteous action
Or fall victim, slowly dying.

The constellations circled back around
The cold embraced me once again
The shining lights that glimmered on the sidewalks
Entranced me to the very, very end
The flame that flickered in my eyes
The silhouettes that blurred the lines
Each sign that whispered through the night
Told of a tale of you and I

Chase each other through the timelines
Your presence lingers in her eyes
She'll pull too deep and send me running
You're left to search both far and near
A scent will hit me as I exit
Intensified with every breath
My knees collapse in the remembrance
Of moments past that flood into my brain

So rock me back and forth 'til I'm asleep
Can't stop the train
Can't leave the tracks
Just find sweet comfort in the melody that beats
On metal lines that parallel and weave
Only our souls define
Whether we live or die

Though the longing may be blue
These fingers keep on strumming through
In wisps the air gets sucked away
Donated from my lungs again
Today I weep and grasp at holograms appearing through my sleep
So close to me yet every reach gets smacked away ungratefully
Stifled, leaking salt back to the sea
One day I'll rise
One day you'll see
One step through time
Is all that I can manage 'til
Aurora finally breaks free
When the sun dogs get released
When split atoms reunite at last
We'll find ourselves
In time
In space
Residing face
To face
Where physics breaks
It's the last moment right before
Creation takes its place

A voice to quiver your heart
A sound no quicker to stop
Flow on to seep into the fabric
Of reality today, will radiate
Each speck of dust
Each cell of mine
No matter where, its true
I cannot hide
Nor would I want with a beauty
So pristine
Clean and passionate
Unwavering

What does it have to take to find a woman to love to cherish and to hold
To share a song from top to bottom
To sing, to play and to behold
A queen among a sea of people
The one that makes me tremble,
Gamble with my dreams and try to hold it all together like escaping steam
on leather
Lean and sexy
Heart of gold and shape of tears
Dammit, where you've been?
I look out to make connection
With your eyes, I get blank stares
So if I'm not the one to find you
Then get your sweet ass out of bed
I've been stuck upon this mountain as addicted as I've been to the empty
space, the silence that you've given me at the beginning
In my time I've carved this mountain
Paved the trails from top to base
Hoping that one day you'll stumble
On a road you'll have to take
One that always leads to me
Sitting on the peak
Alone
Happy
To be free
Come and see me when you're ready
To begin a family

The time we spent alone
However short or long
Has gifted me one thing
Sensations in my heart
No longer numb or dark
Allowing me to dream
Of futures bright
Pure bliss, delight
Romance, a flame that's blinding
Someone to hold
To call my own
Forever walks beside me
Whether you stay
Whether you go
Whether you love
Whether you won't
Neither my heart
Neither my soul
Be torn apart (cus I)
Cus I found my home
Humming along to a
Stranger's song
The distance shrinks away
Connections made
A heart is saved
Illusion of separation's gone
It doesn't take
Much time or faith
Or reason in your mind
To find the one
Who truly feels
Belonging by your side
Whether you stay
Whether you go
Whether you love
Whether you won't
Neither my heart
Neither my soul
Be torn apart (cus I)
Cus I found my home
I found my home

Who could foretell
What would transpire
The moments after our first kiss
A burning fire
A sparked desire
Of sapphire drying on my lips
I picked you up and checked you out
That night I could not sleep one wink
You had me struck just by your covers
And then the ink inside of you would sing
Each passage filled with gratitude
Each word would reach my soul
Without your pillow whispers in my ear
I would have never know this hope
Your story filled with endless love
Each sentence ended with a kiss
I read between your every line
And carved your chapters on my chest

I dream of a world where you and I
Can learn so easily
Where kids will be allowed to fly
Where no one has to be afraid to learn
Where chances given, respect is formed
Where nothing needs to be enforced
'Cus fun of learning will surpass
And growth of mind will let you pass
Onto a plane of limitless creation
And you will find no reason for impatience
For all creations take good time
They take your effort, your brilliant mind
One day it will come back to you
One day it'll all fall into place
The puzzle pieces will race
To take their shape
And form each day
To be the one you've felt before
A magic land that gives you more
Of peace and love and satisfaction
It brings you forth to the attraction
Of every thought you once had had
All of the good, all the of the bad
And with it, contrast that will shed
Creative aspect of what you've laid
Upon your life from the beginning
They come to pass for you my darling
Just give to us a little effort
A picture never seen before
Just live your life without restrictions
Just go for it with all of your
Might and strength and courage fostered
I promise you, it will be there
When you require that little extra push
It all will come from your inside
The power courses through your almighty mind
It brings you closer to abyss
Of endless wonder and pure magic
Just send you love, sealed with a kiss

I was blinded by the light
You were hiding in plain sight
I was trying to reclaim my life
You walked in through the door and you
Set my heart on fire

I took your hand and you took mine
We went along the river bend, and you smiled
I thought your beauty was beyond divine
A star disguised in human form
Bring me to life
Too soon I recognized the signs that I should go
My fears materialized in the mirror that you hold
Thought I could give you my heart, make it your home
But I, I proved myself wrong
I was wrong, I was wrong, I was wrong
So many years have gone by
The ground had vanished in mid stride
I caught the culprit of these crimes
And now, I just wish we could go back
To you and I, you and I, you and I
I just want to apologize
I just need to apologize
I wish I knew
Just ask the moon

What a moment
What a time to be alive
Walking side by side with wolves
Ruby sparkles, lean and full
Smiles fill the atmosphere
Twinkles gleam
Our hearts may sing
For the chance of being here
Evening marches on to star fall
I now know what it's about
Dancing in the moon lit rain
No more worries
It's ok
Hold my hand and float in darkness
Tame this moment, make it stay
Couldn't promise you a future but I'm giving you today
Everyday
Seconds add to fill this space
Walls once bare
Afraid to open up and share
Screaming louder than the pain
That I once felt
Longing for you scent
For the chance to look you up and down
Take you in, exhale, and drown
Moan the night away in pleasure
You and me, once more, together
Put the pieces back in place
With my hands, your hands embrace
Lace my heart up, like my shoes
That walked miles to get to you
Face the truth that kept us separate
Deep inside, I knew you meant it

Bewildered by the sight
Of sparkled starry eyes
The song sang soft and gentle
Inside my heart
You couldn't tell
The lava rising through the mantle
You turn around
I catch a glimpse
My heart did stop
With thoughts of romance

I don't know why but in my mind
I couldn't shake the feelings of
Familiarity and sights of you and I
Being acquainted times before
Believe me that my focus was drawn
As tensely as a bow and arrow
A diving sparrow fishing for its only meal
Delivered from the depths of hell
Desire, passion, ringing bells
The oldest chapter in the book
A spell of love, attaching hooks
That pull me in, seductive looks
Like glancing straight into the sun
Oh but one second at a time
Can one appreciate the soul
Of love began so long ago

I'm but a man who finds this love
The final frontier, rests above
A destination in the world, imagination to the masses
Re-invitation to the fool
Who threw bricks stones in loves glass houses

I let it go
After the moment passes
Been burned before
But the emotion last and lasts
We head our way
After our initial phase
That rocked my foundation
The day light fades

And there you are again, and dancing
Your hips they sway from left to right
You look my way, perhaps a subtle invite
Can't help but smile and dance on through
Allow the music to speak my truth
The rhythm rocks me side to side
A subtle glide, a glance inside
She slides in closer just to see
The endless world I've made inside of me

She runs about, just hoping for the chase
Play cat and mouse, but a lion doesn't play that way
I left as soon as the music stopped
Went on my way, did not look back
Sat down to play, a song or two
Of love, of searching, about you

And as I open up my eyes
I see you sitting by my side
Eyes open, gleaming in the night
You touched my heart with just one sight
I felt your beating heart in mind
I sang that love song with all might
Emotions brighter than that light
That blinded me across the campfire
Don't know you or what you're about
Don't know your future or your doubts
Don't know if you've ever had a cast
From broken bones and children's laughter
Don't know the struggles of your life
Don't know achievements of delight
Don't know if you've grown wings to fly
Don't know your feelings, lows and highs,
Don't know a single fact about you
Yet here I sit
Falling so deep
Skipping all sleep
Just to feel one more moment by your side

It's been two days, still haven't said a word straight to your face
Don't want to rush and let it go to waste
I like a saunter kind of pace
A silent phase

Andrey Psychè

The one I learned to savor

But you bring out the hidden shades of love
And though I could, swoop in and sweep you off your feet
For once
This time
I want you to choose me
That's why I place before you distance
I wonder if you'll grow to miss me
That's why I melt when you decide
To sit right next to me all night

It breaks my heart to see you walk away
Not knowing if I'll see the day
Where you and I can run away and play
A game that people play when they're alone
A game of friction
Sweat and moans
A game that leaves the body numb
That leaves it trembling from the fun
Of two whole separates merging into one
No other boundaries can be won
Connections pulsing
Hooks deep inside
The spirits wander
See the divine
Through practice
Jerking tears of life
In throws of passion all through the night
The two collide
A husband and a bride
Not knowing what comes next
Uncertainty abides
But fear no longer lingers here
As you and I lay side by side
No single worry comes to mind
We now reside in a world between the lines
Free to design a life where you and I may bind
Elope and run away
To find our quiet place
Embrace our grace
And after these long days of torture
At last lay down inside our home

How joyous of a time
I find you next to me in line
I decide to give you that which once was mine
A painting of my rights and wrongs
Of breadcrumbs life laid out in plain sight
To see if I can find the path that leads
Most light
An essence of myself not made
That can compare to other one I laid upon you open hands this morning
To make for certain
That you may know
The feelings burrowing down below
Maybe someday, we'll see the golden threads of fate
We will combine the broken lines that brings us closer to the truth
Until that time
Can't run of hide
Just want one thing
To know your side
Although we've had some time to
Be one on one just passing though
The world along our rearview
No focus paid to things but you
It feels so new and yet familiar
Don't have a clue just how I got you here
But now I know I have to see
The depths of your personality
The reason for your smiles
The pain of heartaches you try to hide
The insecurities kept alive
To grow infinitely in life
And how you did what most cannot
To catch my interest
Ignite my spark
Unravel mysteries that prove
Our paths to cross
A new direction free of loss
But 'til this life decides to form
I'll do my best and give you
More emotions buried deep
Sing all my heart for you to see
And find such pleasure that you lay
On that blue blanket, 10 feet away

No sweeter sight I've yet absorbed
No ocean
Mountain
Scenic road
Has held a chance with your sweet glance I see upon your face today

One thing is for certain
I didn't say goodbye
'Cus from this moment on
Your heart it lives inside
I carry it with me though space
Through time, it grows encroaching haste
But just as what I sang that night
You love me pure with all your might
Inside my universe, you will be bright
Shine on my star, shine on your light

BETWEEN

Why do we do the things we do to do or feel the things we feel are real?
What makes the devil up and move to move up to the surface and scratch
his nails against your window?
What stopping you from staying still and face the faces that we are still
afraid of facing in the mirror of our heart or mind or soul for matters make
it worse it matters to un-curse the lover from the holds of chitter chatter
that the devil whispers in to this free space of matter
Shatter the illusion, grant her the inclusion to a world of hearing but not
grieving letting go of hooks deliberately waiting to take hold and pull us
down below.
What is it for?
Just but a silent pinhole in the air that sucks in time spits out free will will
will your might up from the core to sit alone and hear the roar
Of mice run to and fro
Deliver news of nothing more
And fade back down to separate doors
Galore of praise again, what for?

It just seems like every day
I am looking for something
And I hope this time I'll find
The destination in my mind
As long as I can see it clear
Ahead I know it will grow near
Appear in front of my two eyes
My heart no reasons left to cry
Each time I get one more step closer
I know I can't go any further
Each time I see the path grow clearer
The fog rolls in, it turns to winter
Each face I meet, they make me happy
But I can't be your friend, I'm sorry
I move on though, forever searching
I don't know what to do
Открыв глаза смотрю не знаю где Я
Только посторонний здесь стоит
Напротив глядя на меня, не понимая
Куда чудак спешит
Он криком быстро замерзает
Кричу, чудак ну помоги
Ты видишь что я умираю
Закрой глаза и вновь родись
Please just bring me back to the place where I belong
Just don't send me back to all these worlds unknown
I look around and see
this beauty is all around me
There's nothing that I need
I finally believe
Your heart was born complete
Just trust me, just trust me
The sense of peace that you may seek
Is closer than you think
The sense of peace that you may seek
Is right inside of me

There are worms inside their mind
Steal their peace and feed on freedom
Block the gates to heavens kingdom
Force all men to seek out crimes
Causing havoc, blurring lines
Circulating its dark magic
Dreams of nightmares, bleak and tragic
Poison, flowing through their veins
Thoughts of judgment rot their brains
Out the window go all logic

Battle starts when you shine focus
Bring awareness to your wounds
Cease the spread of poison fumes
Gossip feeds the plagues of locusts
Starve the parasite and notice
Love and light begin to enter
Saturate our souls with embers
Set ablaze the world anew
Peace and joy will bloom in you
Illuminate our darkest chambers

And remember, do your best
Every moment that you get
Don't allow your peace be stolen
By the demons of the fallen
Find your center, let them rest
And remember, do your best
Every moment that you get
Don't allow your peace be stolen
By the demons of the fallen
Find your center, let them rest

I've been sorting through this haze
Tripping over my own feet
Getting up and moving forward
With no sight, only by feel
Understanding
Only where I've been
Try to use the echoes wisely
I call out
Can't hear you back
Try a different door or alley
Washed upon the shore alone
Drenched and soaked straight to my bones
On solid ground
Call out once more
A woman comes in fire red
Flowing like wind around my head
God made all roses just for her
Walks up to me
Leans in so close
With hesitation
I confess
I'm only looking for my Grace

Through one hole and out the other
Skipping timelines like some stones
On the surface of the river
That one had like 20 more
Spin and speed are just two factors
Navigation is the problem
Where you end up no one knows
Learn to drive with your eyes closed

There comes a time
Where all the signs are pointing to the middle
When every rhyme
Come from the mind of reason
So please excuse me when I decide to step aside, move to the fringes of the
night and go back to the place that struck me like a bolt of lighting
A place allowing me to howl up to the moon and bring relief to all my
wounds that festered slowly
A place that doesn't have directions
No GPS, no physical location
Only a pure somatic sensation
Projecting outward like the air on a hot day
Escapes the pavement out in waves
It's centered in you
It resonates
Creating ripples through the aethers
Creates the time and space we see
Real shapes and matter coalesces
Into the images we seek
That's why I have to stop and listen
To what my heart just wrote to me
I have to stop and reassess my reasons
For who I am to be
I'll rest here 'til I see
The silhouette I've grown to miss
Mirages coming out to greet me
I hope that one of them
Will be
The one that my heart sings for
In my sleep

Watch me spin around in circles
Fifth time I've been here today
Walking up and down the hallway
A minor resurrected from the grave
I could hear the past collapsing
Structuring the world a new
Birds are chirping
Sun is shining
What was once
No longer hurting
What was done
Long gone forgotten
Now the new gets time to brew

Eyes are open
Heart, asleep
Underneath this blanket, sadness
Tries to melt away its problems
Roll on over, back to sleep
Second time
No expectations
Dreams were bitter sweet once more
Soul is missing truth and passion
Yet, your feet still hit the floor
Setting sail off lonely shore
Even though it can be hard
It's our choices that define us
Persevere and have some faith
What you find, this life, surprise us
Stormy days can bring in kindness
Light breaks through the clouds above
True change happens in one moment
Moment that is housed in love
Past the pain
Follow your comfort
Gold heart echoes back and forth
Find yourself among the living
Up ahead, a challenge, thrilling
With new friends that keep you breathing
Keep you moving, brand new start
Pays to listen to your heart

Each day we rise and fall
Outside of our control
The thermals up above
Will stumble
In and out of your soul
Can fight it night and day
But reconsider if you may
How can you win against this
Immaterial sway in the trees
Change the way of the winds
Avoid the waves of the seas
When, you see
You're but a cork in the ocean
Bobbing up and down
If you just relax
Let go of your commotion
Float up, sink down and feel
Just how divine
Your whole experience
So mean at times, so kind
Is just like the changing of the tides
You rise, you grow, you fall
You do it all again
But with it learn
To be a friend

Seedling sprout surrender sweetly
Over to the light so weakly
Bow as low on knees you grovel
Less than speck of dust you marvel
Fill yourself with divine guidance
Drain the detours to your kindness
From a seed success will slither
Through the cracks the time will bring us
Closer, closer, closer still
To the final moment when, all of it begins
When the darkness got engulfed
When the star dust took its shape
When the lovers reunite
When no boundaries remain
You will find a bed of flowers radiating night to day
Kneel on down beside your brothers, hand in hand will bring us change
Bring a tear
Misplace it somewhere past the eyes
Feed the soil with cries and whales of your hearts long lived tales
Of the battles it endured
Finally to lay down arms
Near your loved ones
In their chest
Hide it all away to rest
Peace attained within your best
Nothing left to beg or fight for
Everything is found between
Fleshy gyrus of these sulci
Radiate, like flowers
Radiate and bring them near
Radiate and let them break
Radiate to give them reasons
To radiate themselves today

Only darkness can caress the light
Only voids can offer growth a space
To rise above the limits set
To shine from wholy places in our mind
To bring us closer to beloved regrets
And bloom aromatize the spark
Each speck a lightning in its right
Bring down the house and let it rest
These wretched bones have seen enough
Intent has always been enough
This heart it weeps inside your dreams enough
To long, to call, to let it know
There's flowers growing in this garden and you might need some beauty for
a change
Well come and open up your arms then
I'm saving all this ripened fruit for you

Throw your words into the fire
They'll be needed not today
Just accept the world's desire
To remain the same
Walk away and keep on searching
Ask your heart which turn to make
Know the place that you arrived at
Hasn't changed

First, experience the realm that's reserved just for the dreamer
Find a purpose in your path
Share the eyes displayed forever
On these walls once bare
Then to find oneself unhurried walking through a view forgotten
Getting pulled by distant past
Find the moment we got lost in
Lost within your stare

Read the answers on the silence
Written by this sunny day
I'm still waiting on that island
Scribbling your name

A spark is hidden
Builds on itself
Two sparks combine will make you melt
Compound the differences without a haste
In time you'll find the sum expands beyond
The notions placed inside your head
You mind feels lighter, free of dread
You see the sparkle in their eyes
No one is separate
All divine
You can imagine how they bind
Into a whole, into one big picture
You'll have to go blind but
With that
You'll find
A love no smaller than the world combined
One step, two step, a thrust, a sigh, relief, a hug, a kiss,
A heart longing recognized
The one in front to be the one
That sparkles brighter than the sun

Past the second hand you'll find
Nothing short of the divine
Freedom that will put to shame
Even their American dream
Melt between this analog
Find yourself begging for more
Move beyond this wretched scheme
And become
But one of few
To see Cosmos from the view
Of infinity perspective
Of what can and will ensue
Of solutions misdirected
And a way to lead you
Through...

Well I'm sitting in the dark
Peering through the canopy
Falling angles
Glowing halos
Wishing only
For my lover
Underneath my breath I chuckle
'Cus
I've said it times before
Seeing love around the corner thinking
What I'd give for you to see me hoping
For more
So let the stars fall
From the heavens
Burn the air that I am breathing
Fill my heart with ashy remnants
Make my tears fall, make my dreams grow, make my fear and make my
pain slow, make my brain stop just
For now
So alarm clock starts to ring
But I'm already gone
'Cus I've been sprinting like a madman
I've been
Running marathons
Been living underwater 'cus I'm drowning in this longing
The only sound I'm watching is this
Watch on my left hand
Share what you reap
You've sewn it so well
So steep yet so fair
My love's always real
Surrounded by colors that shout out my luck
No matter the number, I'll still be your rock
Burn the air that I am breathing
Fill my heart with ashy remnants
Skin my pride and burn the leather no the weather won't stay shallow
Hold my hand when I am sulking
Let me starve when I start jonesing
Don't want to try to fool you, now a king but once a jester

Form is basic
Shaped the same
As the day to day mundane activities of
Rain and wind that gush right past you that
Break the branches on the pastures
It's all there
Nothing has changed
We simply forgot how to look beyond our own face
There's a mirror
There, reflection
Oh my god!
An imperfection?!
Running wild while rest remains
If you want to play the game
All the rules were written in a grain of sand

A moment lasts a century in the heart
My eyes
They quiver
They tear up
All from the truth that spills out oh so sweetly
I couldn't help but stare at you so deeply
I shake
I die
But your somber tone brings me back to life
Your song
It penetrates my life
A love, forever seeking
A want, forever grieving
A soul forever hungry
Can't satisfy the emptiness
But your warm and fluttery sensation
Brought out within me elation
You quickly stole my heart
While you stood here in the dark
Baring your total soul
Eclipsed my heart just so
I know it isn't fair
I wouldn't blink
I couldn't dare
Miss a single second
Emotion or expression
Your words they rang so true
So passionate
So loose
Could not control my action
Fell hard, without your asking
All moment's all it took

There is magma in your arteries
This fire flows within
It's fueled by all your tragedies
Transmuted with your sins
One touch from golden fingers
Can set the lands ablaze
The continents will shiver
From every step you take
This power comes from cosmic rays
From unisons of future days
Alignment pleads within your heart
And purple, bleeds from every cut
Just stop
The current flowing leaves you blue
Sit still,
Let waves roll through to you
She'll visit you and shape your truth
Now disciplined, begin to move.
Be born of fire and of ice
Opposing forces merge inside
The power's given to the mighty
Inside your palm, the future lies
Don't think too hard
Just close your eyes
Your fate has already been decided

Just stop and smell the rose
They'll remind you of your home
And the next time you are dazed, confused
You will need to find that road
Don't forget to look up high
Where the birds are gliding by
Where they dance 'til sun gets eaten
Where they sing to passer-by's
They'll remind you of your nature
So that when you're feeling down
You'll recall the threads that led
On this path and it'll remind
That One road that leads you to heaven
To that state of peace in mind
And you'll stop your bloody worries
Redesigned and re-inspired
Find yourself back at the mercy
Of all that
Which makes the world go 'round

Andrey Psychè

The flight
of this sound
can reach past your ears
Explodes in your membranes
caressing your brain
A whisper that lingers
and spikes up the flesh
No need to fill the silence
the music is near

From chimney to chimney
From world to world
The eye gets wider
To see the whole
One box can suffocate the heart
Asphyxiate the will to thrive
Each jump you make gets easier still
Connecting neurons and worlds until
It all gleams bright, ideas unified
Our box ain't separate
There is no you or I
Zoom out 'til separate
Converge in center eye
Where all the storms find their own peace
Where turmoil sleeps
Where you and I can finally be
And things tend to repeat
To repeat

Judge not by the completion of my skin
But by the character within
You see your story come alive
But understand, I'm not that guy
You take your thoughts and let them roll
I'm but a screen for every soul
To look upon their darkest secrets
Through me you'll either judge or grow
The monster that you see is hidden
The saint you found is all too close
Whatever image you're perceiving
It starts within your very mind
And falls upon the ground
For you to pick it up
But you just look away
It takes just but a second to realize this trash
Is self-contained
It is self-made
Dispose of it and you will save
Not just yourself
But our own mom
For future days

Every boundary you see
Was erected carefully
Each decision was precise
-Where you may or may not pass
There are some who test the limits
Of a person's heart with gimmicks
Push the line a little further
Climb the fence for feeless entry
Scurry side to side
no worries
There's no consequence
Don't worry...
No one else can see
It's blurry...
Get away with murder
Surely...
Just ignore the signs
They're boring...

There's no hiding from the light
In the shadows of the past
You've been bound by false delight
By the comfort of your sorrows
Every prick that pierced the skin
Further drives the point, beloved
Liars come and go like flint
But a flicker in your silence
Balance taught you that the light couldn't live without some darkness
Harness treasures from the plights of each morning that we borrow
Though there's pain and there is suffering
Though the venom runs within
You can stand and fight for something
Maybe one day, you will win
Maybe one day we will win
Maybe that's the point of life
Maybe everything's within

Grinning ear to ear
Jump on in
to murky waters

You've watched me
Fail and succeed
Did we agree?
To get together somewhere else
You and me

You cannot live your life
Without me by your side
But I will see
For you to be
A Majesty, a Queen

I cannot sleep
I cannot bathe
I cannot run
I cannot shave
I'm sitting here, I don't know what to say
I've been pretty happy, recounting my whole day

There's no avoiding life
She'll find you just the same
She'll throw you to the wolves
Return with each one tamed
The fool will say he's ready
At any moments whim
The wise man sits and studies
Accepting death within
It's fear that drives the common plane
Without it, who's to blame?
Observe your courage reappear
Regain control of it and steer
The lessons written very clear
Your driving force is put in gear
And at that moment
Decisions come
What kind of man will you become?
What choices led you to this place?
What have you learned along the way?
What powers hidden in a day?
What universe you found to stay?
And how much impact do you make?
New experiences give new devices
To tinker with lives vices

Oh time
How frivolous you are
How slow you trickle on and on
Cicadas underground

A thing I could not find
More frivolous than time
Having no true direction
Its passing undermined
Our only wish forget it
Displaced it from the mind
Get lost within the moment
Rekindle the divine

Nothing left to recreate
Everything that you have made
Grows from the ashes of the heart you once possessed
In your grasp it had to melt
So that we can witness how attachment to delusions and the struggle to
maintain
Balance, sanity, innately present in our veins can bring down the tallest man
But you mustn't falter now
Standing tall comes with the title
I am me and you are you
There's no compromising that
Even in our foggiest mindset
Where confusion learned to thrive
Even there we find a kernel of our self, trying to hide
Pluck it from the highest branches
Set it back down on the ground
Tell it that you're tired of chasing
Faces
Just be here and settle down
You have found and bound the reasons to exist
There is purpose underneath our very feet
Drill it
Mine it
Refine it
Then
Give it away
Reverse pick pocket and watch them smile for days when they reach in with
their hand
Pulling out a miracle
Planting it atop their former graves
Recapitulates the past and releases all the pain
Let the purity inside feel at home again
Linger there
Craft down a home
If you wanted friends who know you
You must build it, then they'll come.
But for now
Feel love alone

CRESCENT

Each point of data that should rise to point a finger at the lies that we
our self continually prize 'cus it defends our ignorance
Makes zero sense to why we dig in deep, bury our heads and hide
When life is on the brink
In fact we're already past it
Yet we still sit and we debate whether the truth is politically correct
I've made my peace with this absurdity
I'm looking forward to my death
I live in full each every day and nothing stops my breath from coming in
and out, not yet
I do not waiver with self-doubt
I've tasted life with all its nectar
And any day I welcome the eternal specter with a scythe to float above and
take my life
But even then I do my best to share a little of my truth that we should not
sit idly by
While glaciers melt and nature cries for our attentions, we are the wrong
We are the problem, we hold the gun inside our mothers mouth, with every
moment, clench the trigger a little tighter til. it . pops.
If you look away it'll just fade
No need to worry about your place or the part you personally play in the
upheaval of dismay because you see, you didn't cause it did you?
You didn't sign the bills that passed
You didn't force their hand to press on when your auto needed gas
You didn't dump your trash in oceans
You simply throw all yours "away"

It's out of sight and out of mind
You've done no wrong, it's always "They"
They need to this, they need to that, I didn't do it, it's they who must
It's not my fault
I'm in the right
Whatever happens, it's not my fight
They'll reach consensus all on their own and clean their mess in time to
Mourn collapse of all I value
Of the fresh air and waters pure
Of frolicking in empty valleys
Now filled with smog as hell fire burns
"I didn't do it
I swear on God"
Will echo out through every home
And we'll all know in fact you didn't
Stand up to fight for what's your own

The flicker of fluorescent bulbs
Shake the image unrecognizable
Where you came from, where you'll go
Doesn't matter
'Cus the goal is just a mark to aim at
You can miss or you can get the bull
Where the treasure lies is subtle
As the arrow draws itself from quivers
Hastily attaches to the string
Finds a place to rest and reconsider
Which direction's destined for its fate
Bow pulls back, the arrow follows,
Someone's pulling all the string
All you got to do is sit there
Ready for the sweet, sweet,
Release tension, let it go
Soar much faster than before
Where you end up is unknown
But just look around a moment
Hear the whistle of the wind
Pierced by your intents and focus
Drown out any fools that spoke
Up against you or your choices
All of that no longer serves you
You were engineered to fly
Feel the thrill of every second
It could end, just blink one eye
Zooming faster, faster, faster
You begin to realize
It was never bout the target
Never 'bout the cozy quiver
Never 'bout what bow you nuzzled
Never even bout the skills
Of the archer up above
If you believe in that kind of stuff
No
This is it
-It's what you're feeling
In this moment as you fly
The beginning had no meaning
In the end, we'll all just die
But for the lucky that are chosen

Andrey Psychè

That hear voices in the mind
Sharpen them into a point
Pierced with discipline, compounded time
For the lucky few remaining
Craving for the taste of life
Strings are taut now
Bow pulled back now
Hope you're ready for this ride

One way or another
The symbols speak the truth
The cuts and bruises I've accrued
Have given rise to you
The pain and blisters might be screaming
The blood may ripple in a pool
The aches have settled down quite nicely
Within their proper home and place
It's easy to recount the losses, to look at your defeated face
But can you see past all the scratches and find the warrior's hidden grace?
The strength it took to go to battle
To wage a war you couldn't win
To get beat up, to scream and rattle
And still stand tall must be a dream
Yet here you are, all might no glory
Who needs it when you look around
The weak willed bitch and moan 'til morning
But you my friend
You stitch those wounds and pray for more

Looking back
It's not that bad
Yet that cloud that once was black
Still remains and travels low
In the eyesight of tomorrow
Looking back
I could have fought
But the tranquilizer dart had immobilized all action
Thoughts were steered from fear
Not laughter
Pain that no one should endure
Fly away but we must
Not
Falter
Not
Hault
Or
Slow down even for a glimpse
Yes I understand
I understand that I do not
I had battles that I fought
Yours are different that I see
But the lesson still remains
To be
The one
To set you free
To give you wings
Become someone
Some body
Who can look back at the pain
And remain
Un-waivered
Unchanged
Unafraid
To stare it in the face
To demand that fate will change
To create the will to thrive
To give back and to survive
To see all that was and say
I wouldn't have it any other way.

You've left me hoarse from all this screaming
I fall before you on my knees
From years of lonely tribulations
All I can do is beg and plead
I felt the pain that fell upon you
From actions mindless and coerced
My time has come to grow beyond you
This chapter finished, lessons learned
Too long this hamster wheel entranced me
Too young to go out on my own
Through years of silence and surrender
I've let it go and stopped to mourn
The loss of indecisions
The nature of control
The fear of the unknown
And let my wings spread forth
To catch the oceans breeze
Fly free among my loved ones
I've joined my family
Tomorrow might not find us
I've made my final peace
An offering of me to you
Complete, no hidden fees
I'm ready for my medicine
The drug between your knees
I've tasted independence
Allowed myself to be
A man yearns for reflection
To grow beyond his years
No longer chasing specters
Prepared to make the deal

Let my mind be cancer free
On a diet filled with greens
High on doing what you love
No excuses, just hard work
Power through the pounding struggle
It all comes with time and hustle
But remember to stay true
To the you, you knew
To foster through
To fight the weakness
Not the world
Grow to be a tad more bold
Step by step, no looking back
Pull, don't push
Learn to attract
Detach attachment
Attach to that which fuels your wings
Fly when required
Rest when spent and grow your dreams
Focus on moving
Not where you've been
Enjoy each moment
And in the end, you'll win

A coincidence, seeming uneventful and of the norm can spiral in
the wheels of fate to turn and turn
A heart beat that once longed for love and courage
gave rise to flames that scour and engulf the world
A string that's plucked will ring until a hand that moved it
mutes it if it wills, yet
It is the hand that sent it into motion
The hand of love and nurture
Everything a song could be, you made
It gets sent flying from your lips,
But once it left, it find life of its own
Inside the hearts and minds of all who listens

Each step you take
A trap, awaits
You fear, you play their games
In time you question who's to blame
And step away, but love remains
A staircase lets you grow, escape
Beyond the grabby hands of apes
It's Fate
That not tomorrow, but today
You chose to stop, to elevate
Atop you sit and gander down
What pleasure do you get, this crown
Uneven, thorny, even drab
The Earth, she calls to you, "please come back"
It's here, you start to turn a leaf
You learned, you taught and now
You live
You walk around past grief, past anger
You shine true love that's free to strangers
Connection strengthens from your balance
And life does deepen into silence

Only the slave needs permission
To act upon his whims
The free man acts on his wishes
The free man lives life to win
With hopeless eyes you ask for mercy
Please may I have some more
Can't I be happy, why won't you listen
I am a human after all?
Take what you wanted
Go forth, don't fret
The obstacles might make you quiver
It's worth it, I'll put my life upon that bet
You see, with every step that you get further
From fragile bubbles in our mind
We build a fortress in the aether
One that invites the crowds and finds
That when that voyage ceased to challenge
You come back home to rest, reflect
You'll taste the freedom, and strength emerges
To push the boundaries one more time
Each and every single time

A pen in hand
Like swords defend
A mind sincere and kind
Nothing can stop
Determined hearts
Whose destiny aligned
Distractions are aplenty
Impossible to start
Decisions racing through his mind
Try not to fall apart
Electrifying lands of purity and light
It's time and space
That warp your gaze
The mind is still divine
Signs all around
You mustn't fear
Your only task to lead
The truth will surely set you free
It's easy to believe
There's nobody just like you
Although we are but one
The man you were tomorrow
Is the woman you've become
A pen in hand
Like swords defend
A mind sincere and kind
Nothing can stop
Determined hearts
Whose destiny aligned
Our only power focus
Perceive and be perceived
Your hardships made you stronger
Your choices were the steed

The world is yours for the taking
But first you must gather your tools
It's of no one else's interest but yours
Jump in the boat and drop the oars
We're all just overworking fools
Just follow the stream
Stop resisting
Become supreme
Each opportunity given
Step out and learn something new
There is no use in believing the world is out to get you
We want the best for all your future ventures
We want to see success inside your eyes
We want to lead the horse straight to the water
All we want from you is take advice
Believe that we have seen it all
Believed the lies we've all been told
Believed and bled through wounds of thorns
We bled and cried
Our heart and mind conflicted
We fought ourselves
And everyone afflicted
We've spent the night
With bloodshot sleepless eyes
Wishing to give and lead a better life
Clean up our act
Be precious with our goals
Outlast the fight
Collect the hidden gold
Our lives are full of hardships
Of choices to be chosen
Our obstacles require growth
An easy life is not worth living
It's the pursuit that we're pursuing
The ending, something to be loathed
Persistence carries on
And with it, the flame to go on
To fight and move along
Hard lessons to be harder
Decisions more in weight
The changes you'll be praying for
The gaining of one's strength

I tried, oh I tried
To keep you from your darkness
I tried, oh I tried
To teach you to be clean
I tried, oh I tried
You paid me back in heartache
I tried, yea I tried
Got buried in your trash

I know you're not to blame
Your actions were my virtue
I tried to keep you tamed
But you burned hot nonetheless
Buried in this mess
I led myself astray
I know we can't be saved
I tried my very best
But hope it seems so far away

Couldn't see your face
Couldn't see you effort
Couldn't see your grace
Couldn't see at all
Never learned to love you
But lust ran through our blood
Just wanted to posses you
Locked up inside my heart
Should've know this from the start
Beginning held our truth
But the words you said were moot
They were foreign abstract art
But you gave meaning to our youth

And as we lay in bed
Staring face to face
So gently pet my head
You wet your lips and say
Mon petit lapin
Vous avez chuchote dans mon Oreille
Ne t'inquiete pas
Apres moi, tu seras entire

What does it mean to be a man
It's the question of all ages
Always written on lose pages
Washed away like words on sand
No one left to comprehend
Kept it secret from our youth
Lead with flaws and failed to prove
That a man must weather all
To accept the battles call
And stand toe to toe with Zeus

You'll be tested left and right
Is it in you, what it takes?
Knowing life gives us no brakes
Waking up each coming night
Anticipating one more fight
Never getting time to breath
Punches thrown, you duck and weave
Battles may be won or lost
Just remember that you must
Never fear where your heart leads

Echoes resonate in silence
Seniors sit and question why
Opportunity must linger
Work confused and then we die
Not I
Not anymore
Shattered expectations on the floor
Find myself in the exact same spot
That once tortured me
Embarrassed me
Poked and prodded
Tore apart the
Core of wonder
Hearts kept bleeding on the floor
Yet, I pondered
Broken but managed to grow
I see ghost sit by my side
Once so evil I surmised
But as I sit here
Each string vibrates waves of love
Happiness I could have only dreamt of
Possibilities and friends
That could not have even been
Lest I sat inside the mud that arrested me from hugs, got me hooked,
drugged up, locked up, insecure, emotional, fucked up
I keep thinking all about it
But enclosed within a smile
With a light that I can't hide
Tried to drown me, I've got gills
Tear rolls down my face so happy
Rolling down with no disgrace
Pulling with it only pride
There's no options in that time
Give a moment and a lesson
Learned to thrive inside my mind

Lion's den would have you thinking I was prey
but time hasn't room for any lies
I'll assure you I'm the master of this cage
I will not die so easily this time

The love that binds us starts within the fractal of our heart that longed for
sweetness instead it found the bitterness
And so the reaching will begin for someone new, for someone beautiful
and lean to come and enter unannounced to fly right in and save you from
yourself
No luck
You dig and search and throw in hooks
Pullin' up rocks and mossy boots
You keep on bleeding on your clothes
And wonder
How much more
Will I suffer?
But suffering will ever last
As long as we're running from the past
The shadow of our own disguise
Will chew you whole and swallow you alive
Don't run, don't hide, don't even blink
Look dead into its eyes and sing your song
Reach deep and snare
Only acknowledgement will dissipate the fear
Only the moment when you grow a pair will you be free from earthly hells
Sit down and look
Inspect the corners of your eyes
Your nose
Your hips your thighs
And realize you've had enough
Of endless battles and bad luck
You're worth it, all eternal bliss
Locked deep inside
The key? A kiss
From one and only, your true love
Not him or her, or them or us
It's you
It's always been
It'll always be
Accept responsibly and move
One step
Two steps
A leap or two
The time will pass and you will see
Both fast and slow
A light will start to shine in me

-Competition has no place
Keep on moving at your own pace
None of us are in a race
We're all trying to embrace
Who we are down deep inside
Don't be fooled by wealth and gold
You're no richer of the soul
Lift your mindset, think in whole
Quit your whining, walk the goal
Don't get misled by your pride
Cus all we've got to fear
Is the thoughts inside our heads
Don't worry baby dear
You will find your outlet
The secret that you're missing
Is to love all you do
No wonder every moment we're on bliss
So come on though
So many make excuses
Might as well be tying nooses
All you'll ever do is lose it
Hear your demons just amuse them
They will take you for a ride
Insecurities will surface
Hidden pains will e unearthed
You will finally wake the horses
Driving you to grand resources
And experience true life
Cus all we've got to fear
Is the thoughts inside our heads
Don't worry baby dear
You will find your outlet
The secret that you're missing
Is to love all you do
No wonder every moment we're on bliss
So come on though
You couldn't pay enough
So don't even try
The party going on
Is my happiness inside
Don't do it for the fortune
Don't do it for the fame

Can't stand to live in silence
My heart was born to sing

While the veil thins between the dream and the voices seem to peer behind
the curtain
I wonder
What's the reason of my treason
Why chase down the thunder
What's the purpose of my meddling
Maybe I should only saunter
Walk because the walk itself is something that has brought me pleasure
Nap when eyes drag low and the ceiling fan sings my melody in whispers
Why fight it
Why deny it
There's a lesson buried deep
Only problem our perception
Close your eyes and go to sleep
Wake with brand new eyes that gleam
See the world in its perfection
Follow suit and you'll be free
To your final destination

First rung
One step
That's all it takes
Don't worry 'bout the endless climb or your mistakes
For if you want to be up high then you decide to place some stakes
Above the sky to fly all night and soar though space
To feel the freedom, feel alive, to be untamed
You must move up, no matter what, live, give and take
Moving along
Momentum kept
Increased your pace
You're making leaps could do it blind, it's not a race
Your confidence unmatched, no tie, you have such grace
Your war cry, freeze all your foes midstride and get erased
No one can match your undivided light, bright summer days
You'll reach the top, just do not stop, avoiding haste
You're having fun
A chance, you leapt
And missed your place
You slipped and fell, you stopped your grind, egg on your face
I found you on the ground, just laying, full of disgrace
You wonder why, your God, divine, your heart of aces
Would make a fool of you, and cry, you fade away
I'm here to ask you, why my child
You've felt betrayed and lied to
What's easy's never worth your time
Just get back up and you'll be fine
The strength you seek is forged through fire

The world is starving for art
Yet, I can overindulge
Do you
From the bottom of your heart
Leave all the thoughts behind
It's better to be a starving artist
Than to let your soul get rotten
Dropped in, locked up, faded past all recognition
All you need's a little color to bring back your intuition
Step by step
We crawl and crawl
Give us time
We'll show you all

It's easy to get blinded by the beauty of this world
Better learn to walk the streets with nothing but the sense of a woman's
intuitions
Lead the way past where the eyes far gone astray
Not to mention all extensions that led down our human brain
But with practice through molasses every move will bring you grace
And in no time but the present will you join this human race

Don't get it twisted
'Cus it's true
You'll get lost
Trying to find it
See logic has this funny way
To make you out in but one way
In but one matter of your sight
And you'll get locked, no key attached
But if you choose to throw it out
Please, not for good
Just for time being
And let the lub-dub take the steering
You'll find your hazy mind clearing
There's but one path that gets you there
To win
To live
To feel
To dare
You'll see it start to piece along
With that true peace
You'll find the one

Told you I would love you more than any other man
Told you I'd accept you and agreed to hold your hand
Told you, you were beautiful more so each time we met
Told you I can't be with you and now I feel regret
Heard your cry for love, it whistled through my heart
Gave my word to take it slow, Then, I just fucked up
There was magic twinkling in your eyes
Hope behind your smile
Star, in human form, disguised
Your purity of heart inspired
But one thing I know
You weren't my girl
You showed me direction
And broadened my world
Inspired great change
Deterred from great pain
It was your loves intention
It was I who's been saved

A blade of gold
The discipline of souls
Waiver oh but once
Old sharp becomes new dull
And all together
We know that fortune
Favors the bold
And leaves out in the cold
The dreamer and the dunce
Whose lack of action do not mold

The prophecy's been told
All entrance tickets have been sold
The spectacle of everyday
Bewilder all who watch the road
The grimmest of your moments
Combusts your body whole
The ashes of your yesterdays
Unfold, the soldier paved with gold

The phoenix of the water
Will shed its fiery tears
No longer will it hold the weight
Of unforgotten fears

Won't you open up your eyes
All you need to fly is to open up your wings
No one is trying to hide any miracles behind the scenes
It all starts with what you allow yourself to see
You can focus far and wide
Focus on being alive
On a caterpillar crawling, slowly, on a leaf to find its place to rest to change
You can focus near or far
That will show you who you are
Every day the things repeat
Just to tell you in your sleep
How your mind look past the magic that has steeped
And steeped and steeped
I can see your deepest wish
And its granted, just like that
But the only way you'll find is by taking off your blindfold
Breath a minute
Find your center
Build a road just for yourself
Stop on over by the seaside
Take a nap, you've earned your rest
Know that in the moments after
You will stumble on a chest
Open up and look inside it
Everything that you've desired
Sitting, waiting, in one place

Every sound
Every thought
Shake the ground
Shapes the Earth
Just imagine
All this strength
In the vessel
Of one man
What to do
And what to fix
Are there problems in the least?
Leave it be
Hear me say
Save it for another day
As for now
Don't you fret
Try to gain experience

Glowing sun
Asked me once again if I'm alright
Falling down
Leaving trail of bread crumbs on the ground
Follow me
Every step will hurt but you'll be free
At the end you'll see
Every treasure
Every dream
Every lover you've conceived
Every Ruby
Every suitcase
Every road that called your name
All of it passed down to you
Mhmm
Just to show you that the truth
Mhmm
Maybe painful at the start
But believe
Inside dark is where you find the art of living
Let the sun go where it may
Unavailable and grey
Rain drops faster every day
But I remain
But you remain
We all remain
A little different

Spark, ignition, air, destruction
In denial, no instruction
Huffing fumes, corrupted lungs
Let it burn, it's not your problem
Burning down of nature
Pollution of the sea
One thing can save the balance
It's up to you and me
The deity of nature
Is dying from her skin
Corrupted deep into her lungs
She's crying from within
Malignancy runs rampant
Her future looking bleak
Billions observing
She hears a final screech
With death and deception seen in every direction you must chose what is
done onto you
To turn a blind eye and to suffer inside or to stand up and fight for the
truth
One soul denies the fallacy
One soul does not accept
One soul ignited by the truth
Responsibility in hand
To have the balls to have a heart to stand behind the truth
No matter the popular belief, you have the right to chose
To bite the hand that feeds you
Burn all the bridges too
To turn your back on everything
And build the world anew
To turn your back on everything
And build the world anew
With death and deception seen in every direction you must chose what is
done onto you
To turn a blind eye and to suffer inside or to stand up and fight for the
truth

The seed will sprout
Just give it time
Regard its growth
With just one eye
As spring gets closer
So will I
Be found in darkness
Prepared to fly
The sound inside my head will bring
Each piece I've come across in time
And one by one to reassess
Beliefs I've clenched to oh so tight
Each one has brought me its affaires
With piercing gaze it moved me through
No jokes or laughter, sitting here
It's time to go
It's time to grow
Time to
Go back and start again, anew
Tabula rasa left to move
Away from grip that holds too tightly
From colors that restrict my sight
Back to a place of utter freedom
A place not housed in space or time
Short legless travel up the bean stalk
And lie there still, no fear of dying

In moments that no longer stack
Just pulled to length of endless stature
Feel heaven underneath my hat
And dance my dance in total rapture

I think I'm ready to evole
Click click click
There is no place like home

I drop down to my knees
No longer feeling pain
The world around me fades to black
My thoughts, I can't refrain
From wondering how I found me here
From thinking what went wrong
Suspecting foul play at hand
And then a silent cheer
Can't see where from
The cheer had come
It must be in my head
I see a little kid run towards me
Returning me from dead
He said it's you or me
We both can't be alive
The happy little, jovial kid
Had managed to survive
With my last breath
I cursed his name
Escaping from that body
A boy who's now been weathered
By battle, pain and money
Returns back home to start a new
With light with joy and laughter
Awaken from a living nightmare
To find a happy ever after
With one deep breath and high pitch hum
I was finally free of the monster I had become

SHADOWS

Every scar you see upon me
Once was festered and inflamed
Blamed my enemies
Curse their names
Hate was flowing through my veins
Pulsing
Rushing
It engraved
Every action with a ink stains
A taste of plain old bitterness would sink
Disdain deeper, stop to think
Don't worry mama
The grim reaper never comes for those that kick the sand in faces of the
kids that lost their hope, cry and moan while I
Smoke and drink my pain away
There was nothing more to say but
Stay away
I'll bleed on you until the day
The wounds that gaped received my eye
My care, my tenderness
Dissolve the blame game for a time
That never comes again
What's done is done
You can't turn
Back
You have power in the now

To heal your wounds and cease the reckless carnage that would end your
spirit's path
Return to sadness and allowing self to feel and mourn the loss of the
innocence and roam about the graveyard seeing all the monsters that have
once belonged
To this body
To this heart
And decide that it must stop
We are human after all
Folly follows us along
But are capable of heights
Unencumbered by the sky
Flying straight through darkest night
You and I
We have the strength
To illuminate the death and pain and start to create again
Once more using what we have
Hold it dear inside your arms
Love it, cherish it
Even if it's not perfect
Especially if it's not perfect
'Cus the one thing that's been missing
From its essence that's been keeping it from endless grace
Your soft heart
Is your firm presence
Your compassion and your ear
Listen
To your aches
Your fears
Shed a mask, put on a tear
This is powerful I promise
Try it out if you so dare
Unbecoming feels like dancing with the Devil down in Hell

Had these demons plague my dreams
Why I asked? They wouldn't answer
Poked and prodded
Wouldn't let me sleep
It was easy to respond in violence
But they wore familiar masks
They wore faces of my loved ones
Yet I still could not excuse their behaviors in that moment
Wretched beast I tell you leave
But it won't, it just keeps going
Running doesn't help one bit
They just chase and grow in numbers
I just want some peace and quiet
But I run, try to survive
Finding solace in my mother
For one moment, someone hears my cries
But, it doesn't last
With a vacuum, half asleep,
I traverse the country side
In my grandpas truck who's driver tries
To lock my seatbelt tighter, tighter
Trapping me but I'm too clever
After decent conversation 'bout the family at home
I escape the demons clutches
Jumping out of his window
Only to be found amongst cave of black and pointy hands, quick a fruit
stand on my right, maybe citrus can defend me
And it did
For they were angels
They brought peace back to my soul
Demons ran and hid in panic
'Cus now I had chose to chase
Throwing juices that would hurt them
'Til I found that even this
Was no better than the latter
Only way to find true peace
Is forgiveness of the matter
With it
I could sleep,
Side by side with angels, demons
I could love them both the same
Never ask either to change

Know their nature
Dissipate the blame
Don't get caught inside the chasing
Just make sure your heart is pure
Move with grace in all directions
All's forgiven
All is whole

Knock
Though the veil may be thin
Knock
And our eyes are filled with sin
Knock
Each adjacent plane affects us
Knock
Glares upon us from within
Knock
We can still find ways to cope
Knock
By exploring past our scope
Knock
By distracting every thought
Knock
With the echoes of our heart
Knock
And we'll find our way back home
Knock
By this one distinctive tone
Knock
Clear the chatter all around
And in time
You will be found

Smell of gasoline has followed me for weeks
Was it something 'bout the drive to be
Somewhere else but here
Not a pleasant smell or texture
Robs the brain cells of its structure
Yet I sit and ponder deeply
Why this smell and
Why me
Sulfur comes around and slaps me
Demons must have come to play
No idea where they're getting
All these tortured souls to pray on
Weak and feeble
Giving handouts of their flesh
I don't blame them
It's their nature
Only we can stop the pain

Must have pissed somebody off
I can smell the smoke from cauldrons
Witches brewing
Gases fuming
Heads been booming
Yet another headache comes
Sunspots could have been the culprit
Knock the grid down on its face
Every piece of electronics
Melted
Shattered
Begged for mercy
Laughter filled the cabin air
No such thing for you my dear
Suffer, squirm and understand
It's the beginning of the end

The mind has long forgotten
Its attachment to this brain
And it went along the trail
To locate the things it can't attain
The abstract emotions linger
Long past feelings overdue
Ears are perked with numbing silence
Catching whispers floating through
In between the land of living
And the land where spirits roam
I will find myself believing
Oneness, unity untold
With it, nothing else can hold up
Flames that flicker, bleeding light
Within, sunshine won't be missed
All I need I've got inside
All I want I've got inside

On the cusp of all and none
Grasped by fear, can't turn and run
To run
You can stand, one foot over the edge
Just waiting for a gentle breeze
What's physical was left behind
The pain of torture underlined
A whole was ripped in one blind eye
To let the darkness fill the sky with stars of light and selfless plight
Inside your sorrows
Tomorrow lends a helping hand
Ill borrow moments to pretend
The horse I led through every bend
Lays flat
Gunned down
By my two hands
The love you feel is all too real
She's waiting on the other side
You close your eyes and fall right in
The time is here
The place is now
So come on in

Salt crystals floating in the air
Fresh salmon swaying through the wind
The sun beams down between my fingertips
This moment I will always keep
Tremendous thunder rolling down the hills
My heartquake match the shaky ground below
Black crows get swallowed by the darker skyline
Engulfed by fear I've never felt before

Run
Can't stop go turn around
Run
It's do or die
Run
Shake off the charcoaled flesh
Run
Run, run for your life

Young diamonds permeate my lungs
I pray to Venus, keep my mind afloat
Emotions flood my body and I realize
The rescued team has lowered down its rope

Allured by sweet aroma captured
The butterfly within your heart
Promises of love longed after
Made you a puppet from the start
Each hook impales the flesh with pleasure
A form of ecstasy untamed
Every wound, it leaks, an essence you once sheltered
With time, your soul, grows weak and maimed
And if you stay
Prepare to lose in every god forsaken way
Yet only the pain
Will teach you love, for self, again.

See the colors in my words
When I say I came alone
Came to finally shake off all the cobwebs that have grown
On these bones since winter started
On this heart since you've departed
Yet I hold you close and dear
Near my heart, along the pier
Sitting silently beside me
Gazing past our heartache's hold
Hold your hand as you remind me
That true love was never told
To be pretty or exciting
To be honest or complete
To be faithful, even solid
Just to make you feel some thing
Just to make you breathe again
Just to make you bleed again
Just to make you cringe and crumble
Cry and carry all your weight
Just to make you call at night to say I love you
Just to open up and sing
Just a simple look of pity that has left a hole inside
Just the willingness to bury all the past,
Beside tonight
I felt your familiar essence
I could spot you from afar
Good to feel that playful laughter
One I helped to disembark
Though I said it through and through
All I wanted was to help
Time reveled to me the truth
I just never listened
Never gave you time of day
Never let you lead the way
Always masked behind my vision
Of my anima in you
Never gave you chance to flutter
Chance to hold it on your own
But I'm happy to discover
That you've made it all your own

You're on the road
No getting off it
It's dark all to your left and right
You keep on moving
'Cus rest wasn't a thing you're taught
No time for stopping
We're running late
We're quick to get to our own graves
The headlights beaming
White lines deceiving
You pass a deer in your rear mirror
It's eye gleam bright from license plates
As if your future gets reflected
Upon the eye balls of this beast
As if its nature redirected
The road you choose to take tomorrow
Its gentle strut and peaceful manner
Begin to crawl inside your guts
You sense a change turning inside you
Attuned with intuitions breath and thoughts
If you would listen
All would be different
You'd find yourself traversing gaps
But more than likely
You'll shake it off
And hit deer Bambi with your car

Taking hits
From every side
Must have been the storm that's brewing
From the windows, to the drive
To the voice that lingers, soothing
Closed my eyes and dropped to mono
All the melodies that rang
Nothing short of talking now
Couldn't muster up the strength

'Cus this wall endured enough,
no more handouts,
box it up
And the pump had given out
So much for the ins and outs
Maybe it's because I gave too much
Maybe it had lowered my defenses
Maybe someone had a crush
And crushed all my pipes of fine-tuned tension

Electricity stopped flowing
Gas decided to dry up
But the pressure kept on growing and destroyed all that I had
Like an empty husk it sits there
Wailing, waiting, whispering
What would wasteful wrinkles wonder
While we watered
Our delusions
Let them grow and let them foster
Whip out vines from every side
Slash your tires, growing brighter
It's just fear you let reside
It's a blessing what I've witnessed
Words can't rearrange or bind
No more shackles, no more burdens
Once I start, you cannot hide

Slow and steady wins the race
Yet the light that's in my face
Blinds the fear that found its way
To each crevice of disgrace
Lord please help before it's late
But my hope and faith have dwindled
Swindled by the gore and plight
Not the monsters that roam freely
But the ones they got inside
Holy shit
You're just a baby
How'd you end up so disfigured
I'm not qualified to say
But your actions and your words are projections of your soul and the image
that I see
Doesn't please me, not at all
Yet you run up to the scene, scream profanity and think all you have to
offer stands in the holiest of lands
Check yourself
So many fools
You all think you know it all
Toxic, cocky, insecure
Trembling within those shoes
From that wretched place you lead
It's disgusting what you bring to the table
Please go home
Sit in silence
Ponder long
And then maybe you'll accept
You're and idiot and then
Only then
Will the world start to unravel
And you'll see your actions grovel
For forgiveness
For a tear
For redemption
For the honor
To be here
Let's not shy away from mirrors
'Cus you fear to see your face

Each word that slithers down your tongue
Glides past your teeth into their ears
It strikes the anvil, on it goes
To change the structure of
The flow of consciousness it touches
The river slows but never stops
The burst of colors that ignite
The forests
Freckles
And our hearts
These words may carry feeble meanings
But with them shape our world anew
Inspired action led the worthy
To take the throne
To cast the stone
To be the first to roam in heaven
No room for cowards, only strength
They die a million times too many
But us
Not even once
You can't deny that all your weapons
Have made you weak down to your core
We have our voice, that's all we need
Prepare for battle, this means war

I'm done convincing, holding hands
My heart can't take your arrogance
You think I'll feed you 'til you die
You think you'll drain me thin and dry
I couldn't care for you to whither
But it's your choice, nor do nor try
Without your wishes, who'll deliver
Your life, will surely be a tie
Can't lose, can't win
Just float in numb indifference
Be carried by the wind
Can't say or do
A thing for one own self
Can't run away
Can't stand or fight
You're powerless inside your mind
And if you chose to remain stagnant
Your will of power will not magnet
Attraction only works one way
The things you want will float away
The things that haunt
Forever stay
And then you wonder how and why
Nobody cared, no body tried
But we were with you through and through
For every choice you chose to do
For every pitfall and mistake
We tried to help you, motivate
But all you wanted was to fail
'Cus it was easier to bail
But now you sit before your God
Just want forgiveness, released from thought
With pain and suffering to spare
Wondering
If life is worth living
I hope right there and then you find that missing piece
And hear us, see us, screaming please
But I have seen this dance before
And sadly, you will experience more
'Cus death is easier than sleep
You drift away and stay for keeps
What no one told you is that life

Will be the hardest battle of your life
Only the mighty can survive
The rest will perish so pick your side

The pain is blinding
Can't catch a breath
Just want to sleep
And leave this mess
Each time I do
I get but just a taste of sweet relief
No sooner still, my eyes unshut
The pain flows through them
To cripple me once more
Fillet me open, and let my innards flow
Take out my spine, rid me of my blood
There's nothing that can ease it
There is no hope nor trying
Each time I think of moving
I find myself paralyzed
I know with time
This too shall pass
And I will feel myself
But times slow slither
Is agony at best
Each second, tic
Each minute, toc
A mallet driving nails inside my head
As if it's trying to unlock
A hidden message in my psyche
But oh the pain is just too sharp
I can't help but crave an end

Hair is rustling past my vision
From the gossip of quiet trees
Lilly pads grab my attention
And the changing of the leaves
Hopping to the sounds of crickets
Chirping snare drums heard at last
Leave me here 'til I expire
Let me take my final breath

Ballerina sits pretty in pink
Regina's specter beautiful and wise
Inside her eyes reflects a vial of black ink
Decides her last words before she says goodbye

So young, she claims so bold
About each lie she's yet been told
I'm done, she screams, the menace of this chapter
Denies past tense, but dreams of the forever after

The wonders of this world are fleeting
Each day brings that which is worth deleting
Hoorays have past the worst is yet to come
Hand full of pills, make peace with your mom

Eternal slumber, snoring Snorlax never moves
It's easy to let go, relax, there's nothing left to lose
Nocturnal wailing gets soothed by numbing blows
Just please her senses raw, releasing all her woes

Her thoughts at altitude of airplanes
She fights, can't ground her with your truth
Subconscious actions run away like freight trains
Last things she hears before she fades away
Samson

Dark clouds
They saturate the sky
You stand and pray for rain
But nothing comes and you remain the same
A single drop will do
To wash away the pain
For reasons unbeknownst to you
The weatherman was wrong today
And with each sunrise, your hope remains so high
The sky remains the limit
You wish to soar and glide
But these dark clouds
They block your visions through and through
Can't see if what you're doing
Holy
Or putrid
Have no clue
I know it never lasts
Time makes fools of all
But God, it feels so heavy
Each time I try to run, I barely crawl
Momentum's all that matters
Which way am I to go
Don't want to slide into a ditch
Don't want to fall flat on my face once more
The endless search, of a soul, awakened from deep slumber
The hollow stare, a torch, in tears, a pointless walk in rainless thunder
A missing piece, it's felt across the whole
But what it is, not you, not I, can ever know
Stumble, step by step, you roam as if dead
Man walking, skip the talking, mumble, groan
A leap from deathly throne to throne
The exit sign shines brightly red
We still have ways to go before we rest
In bed, we wish to stay for good
This mood, it's easy to forget, to lose my appetite
For food, for anything sustaining
Just thoughts of brain, of heart
Of filling holes that have no start
No end, no edges, blackness, hunger
Only the journey will remain
All else consumed by naked flames

No use for us, no weight, no gain
From which, on this day, perhaps the future or the past
To will reclaim, the piece that you have lost
And once again, you'll roam the planet free
From any worry, bestowed with glee
Departing clouds and dry the rain
Of people desperate, charred and pained
There's always hope, no matter weak
Just take your time, just try, even if you need to
Cry yourself to sleep

Heart open from the start
Our eyes they met at dusk
My lonely days are gone
A memory from the past
You offer me your hand
I take it soft and gentle
With time my grip turns solid
You quickly turn resentful
I try to offer love
And keep you close to me
But it becomes apparent that
You are no longer free
A flower that's been picked
A bird, locked in its cage
I try to wrap my mind around
Your new malicious ways
You leave me broken hearted
I try to call, you don't
This finishes the story
Of the boy who loved too strong

I have found there's but one way to allow the world to change
Step aside and close your eyes, stop observing for a while
Speak your peace and make it so
But you have to let it go
No sense staring at a wall
Time will pass and hope will grow
Maybe it's the cowards way but I see no way to change the heart of every
man, woman, child or alien to think deeper for themselves and release their
grasp of all their sins
Action they chose every day to go up against their fate, their best nature,
their own God, because why?
Because they hurt?
'Cus your president said so?
Still can't hear you, 'cus you're mad at you mommy and you dad?
'Cus you drink your life away, feel a bruise, forget the day you received it
and move on
Call it crazy
Stick to your guns
Know that no-one will or wants to caress your dirty wounds
They've done the work
They've put to bed
Their own demons, now their friends
So all it is, a waiting game
We let go of yesterday
Have no future in our brain
Double down on here, today
If we die, then let it be
It was written in the stars
But at least we lived with heart
I will not participate
In your game, let's call you winner
I'll be making a new game
Yes it true the old one sucks
No I won't invite you neither
Have fun yelling at these rocks
No one wants to feel your anger
If you change, then we can talk
When you grow, then we can talk

The monsters that you fear so much
The ones that you wouldn't dare to touch
They're free of all that you posses
Free of the torture in your head
Free, to act or do or will
To choose their destiny and thrills
To be among their family,
Their kind will always thrive to be
Accepting where each draws their line
No need to push or pull each other
They see that freedom isn't bothered
By peoples feeble tries to slaughter
The ones around for their own gain
'Cus they have yet to see real pain
The pain that makes a man stand taller
The boy gets killed, emerges stronger
They know that one day it will come
Just shake their heads and let them run
You try but all your efforts fall
Allow authorities to come
And hit them over with their guns
Perhaps it's now they'll understand
You hope but guarantees are dead
Avoid it and move with your life
You made your mark
You did your part
Now rest with ease
Relax, relinquish, and restart

Whisper, whisper, in the night
You may want to stand and fight
But you lost before you entered
All that waits is your demise
Tears are falling
Children crying
Grown men calling on the phone
"Mama save me, please don't leave me in this hellhole all alone"
We, the pines stand tall and silent
Waiting
Plotting
Your next fall
Don't come back lest you desire
To feel pain of tortured souls

Quiet giants standing tall above the public seeing all there is to see
No more falling for the first approaching woman, child or man that comes
across their path to wake
Or break their inhibitions there's a plan behind their actions
Let the feeble move unnoticed so the strong may have their day
It's not too late
I have realized that of late
Time takes pleasure in the wait
Even if we like to squirm
Balance brought this life from dreaming
Falling down no longer hurts
Float on over
Wings of passion
Try to hold on
While we shift

Thoughts of little minds to show off ignorance
And bark your insecurities, I smell your impotence
A little boy just running scared
From every monster living underneath your bed
Perhaps there'll be a place someone has structured
With castle walls and guards on duty
Truly, a place that feels like home, you keep on pushing, on your own
But you break in and get kicked out
No one desires you around
They chase you out each time you're seen
The cops get called, arrest the fiend

The question enters once again
So why can I not find a reason to remain
This moment seems to think itself as vain
You try and try and try again
But to what means
What can you change
This world will fight you tooth and nail
To stay the same
They all have the answers in their brain
They know it all and you're just a waste of space to them
You want to help and give them something past their reach
But in their face are looks of pride, contempt,
They don't need you, you don't need them
Can you feel the pain rush through your veins?
Your heart bleeds blue, you gave them all your air
But do they want it anyway?
I heard that any fool can learn from ones mistakes
A sign of wisdom is to learn from others
So what's your place
In presence of this day
Where people spit in each other's face
Can't tie their shoes but speak of moving mountains like it's what they do
They don't need you
They need to feel the bite that only failure of life can slip inside their food
A drop of poison in the soup that they've been stirring in themselves
Only tasting the bitter sweet defeat
Got kicked around, lost a few teeth will they look up and see the truth
But will it be late?
It's not for you
To worry

Only fear what you don't know
From a distance
Strong resistance
To connections that we hold
There is more to you and me
More to love
More to reprieve
Nothing but the space around us
Fill it up with what you please
Leave the judgments past your grasp
All they crave to do is hinder
Your experience to fullness
Warmth and love in middle winter
A modality of totality in reality we lead
Grows too certainly, emotionally, engrossing our need to see
Adjust your focus little tighter
Pull your face a little closer
Analyze and learn to know that which harnesses beliefs
Realize that in this seed
An epiphany, a leap
To a world unlike your own
One that yearns to understand
Gives compassion, lends a hand
Love passed freely and you see
There was nothing here
To fear
Just a terrible reflection
In dark waters of black seas

Without the darkness
The light would hold no meaning
The pain that we are feeling has a place inside out heart
Heavy feet
Shuffle onward with a glooming sense of failure
Wouldn't it be great if we just let it fall apart
Springs are loose
The screws are missing
Nut I tried was way too small
What's the point of my own screaming
When your audience is earless
Closed my eyes to find a shelter
Melt inside the dark abyss
Loss of boundaries gave me something to hold near
All for one and one for all felt like just another phrase 'til you find yourself
alone breaking pieces off yourself
Well just break then into silence
Shatter it into mere dust
Let me float off to the distance
Getting lost
'Til I can find a mold that suits me
'Til I can see above the stars
'Til I can live among the darkness
Holding hands with those I love

Sick and tired of these words just making sounds and not much more, it's action that can change it all so take a pause and put the words away for now and see what really comes to grow out of the silence and the boil of the frustration of being somewhere where you feel like you do not belong
"So long, farewell, auf Wiedersehen, goodbye
I leave and heave a sigh and say goodbye"

ABOUT THE AUTHOR

Andrey Psychè, also know as Andrey Pavlenko was born in Magnitogorsk Russia in 1991. His family migrated over to the United States in 2002 which allowed Pavlenko to experience an whole new world, new perspective, and gain opportunities that would otherwise be hidden from his life. Initially, Pavlenko set off to explore the scientific world, placing his trajectory toward becoming an MD, but after completing his prerequisites, earning a B.S in Biology from the University of Washington and working with a doctor for over a year, he declined his offers to attend Medical School and found himself in the middle of a custom manufacturing business his mother owned and operated. By applying the same learning techniques he used in school, he quickly taught himself how to program and run CNC machinery which broke the seal on whatever was keeping his creative juices bottled up, allowing a brand new life to pour out, birthing Andrey Psychè. Psychè began his work very modestly with small engravings. After a deciding he wanted to see what he could create without using fancy tool and solely rely on himself, he picked up a bucket of paint, started flinging pigment onto whatever would accept it, stumbling across creation which depended largely on the complete loss of control. This played hand in hand with Psychè's new lifestyle of mediation, health, and inner work which reflected itself to him in the abstract composition of his paintings. This led him to translate his first painting into his first book, "Expedition of the Psyche" revolved around ideas of philosophy, psychology, and self improvement. He continued to evolve his visual art, always striving to expand upon what he has already achieved. He learned that you can reuse the same art for inspiration, to dive deeper and expand on what is already present. He learn how to become his own muse and later went on to stumble upon music. He learned guitar and began putting his new means of expression to use by writing his own songs. He still credits his rapid growth in music and songwriting to his understanding of the abstract principles that his paintings taught him. "Art is art, whether it's paint or music, they share the same fundamental processing that allow the artist to interchange the same techniques between disciplines, which at the same time reflect life itself."

Psychè now spends his days teaching in various schools, passing on his knowledge of art and his understanding of his own life onto the youths of tomorrow, hoping to influence in any way the next generation to keep certain qualities of thought in their mind. He says there is nothing more creative in this world than sculpting the mind of future generations, and if we are to evolve as a society, the answer is and always will be in education.

Through art, we can learn much about the artist. Through the artists, we can learn much about ourselves. Though ourselves, we can learn much about the universe.

Made in the USA
San Bernardino, CA
12 January 2019